Prepare If You Dare

A Halloween Scare in IRELAND

To my own little monster, Max, and his marvellous mum x

Visit the author's website! http://ericjames.co.uk

Written by Eric James
Illustrated by Marina Le Ray
and Natalie & Tamsin Hinrichsen
Designed by Sarah Allen

This edition published by HOMETOWN WORLD in 2016
Hometown World Ltd
7 Northumberland Buildings
Bath BA1 2JB

www.hometownworld.co.uk

ISBN 978-1-84993-782-5

Printed in China
HTW_PO020616

10 9 8 7 6 5 4 3 2 1

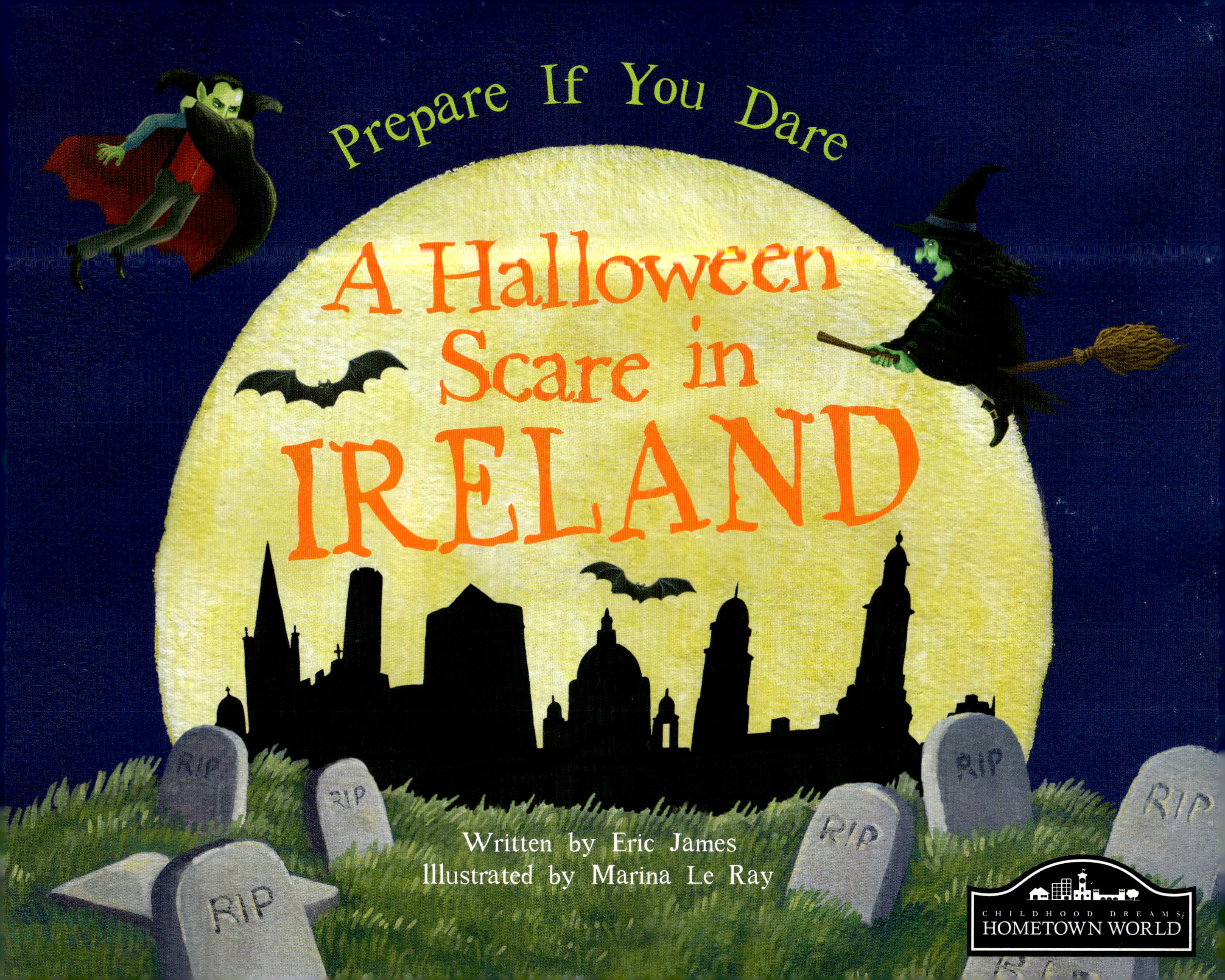
Prepare If You Dare
A Halloween Scare in IRELAND
RIP
Written by Eric James
Illustrated by Marina Le Ray
CHILDHOOD DREAMS
HOMETOWN WORLD

Prepare, if you dare,

for a **big Irish scare**,

A night of pure terror to whiten your hair,

A tale full of sights that are best left unseen.
'You ready? 'You sure?

This was my Halloween...

The werewolves
howled loudly.
The moon shone so bright.
I stayed in my bedroom,
the curtains shut tight.

My heart started pounding,
my knees felt so weak,
But, being a brave kid,
I just **had** to peek.

I pulled back the curtains. My mouth opened wide.
An army of monsters had gathered outside!
They staggered and stumbled and lurched down the streets
With bags full of lollipops, chocolates and sweets.

Emerging from sewers and alleys and drains
Came creatures and critters with cravings for brains.
And more came to join them from places nearby,
On buses, on broomsticks, by road and by sky.

From Dublin to Belfast and Limerick too,
A mountain of monsters, the motliest crew,

All gathered together
for one spooky night,
To seek out the living
and give them a fright.

The thunder clapped loudly with terrible booms.
The witches dodged lightning and clung to their brooms.
The two-headed doggies tried chasing their tails,
And banshees let loose with their hideous wails.

The vampires hung out
on the street in their gangs,
And grinned, just to show off
their pearly white fangs.

The mummies moaned loudly and swayed side to side,
While Frankenstein stomped about town with his bride.

The Newtownards ogres arrived in the night,
Determined to give everybody a fright.
They climbed Scrabo Tower and hid out of view,
Then jumped down to scare passers-by with a "BOO!"

The leprechauns came into Dublin one night.
And gave poor Medusa a terrible fright.
They told her they'd heard that Saint Patrick was near...
To see all the snakes on her head shake with fear!

The creepies were crawly, the crazies were crazed,
The zombies from Sligo had eyes that were glazed.
The ogres from Wicklow were as ugly as sin,
With big bulging noses and warts on their chin.

The ghouls danced around but were lacking in soul,
The gargoyles could rock, and the headless could roll!
Although the whole spectacle seemed to spell doom,
I foolishly thought I'd be safe in my room!

But then something happened
that made my heart jump.
From somewhere below me
I heard a big **THUMP!**

I froze for a moment, as quiet as a mouse.

Yes, I could hear noises from INSIDE THE HOUSE!

I put on my slippers

and pulled on my robe.

I shook like a leaf

but I don't think it showed.

Then, slowly but surely,

I crept down the stairs,

Preparing myself for the
biggest of scares.

LEAP CASTLE

My hands trembled wildly.
I opened the door.
I still shudder now
at the horrors I saw.
The stereo spat out
some hideous sounds
As dozens of monsters
jumped madly around.

The sight was horrific. It made my skin crawl.

These monsters were having their

Halloween Ball!

And right in the middle, one monster loomed tall,
The **hairiest, scariest monster** of all...

He turned round and saw me.
I fell to my knees.
"I'm not very tasty,
so don't eat me, please!"

He beamed ear-to-ear
and broke free from the huddle,

Ran over,
and gave me a...

BIG

MONSTER

CUDDLE!

"At last!
We have found you!" he said with a smile.
"From Derry to Kerry
we've looked for a while.

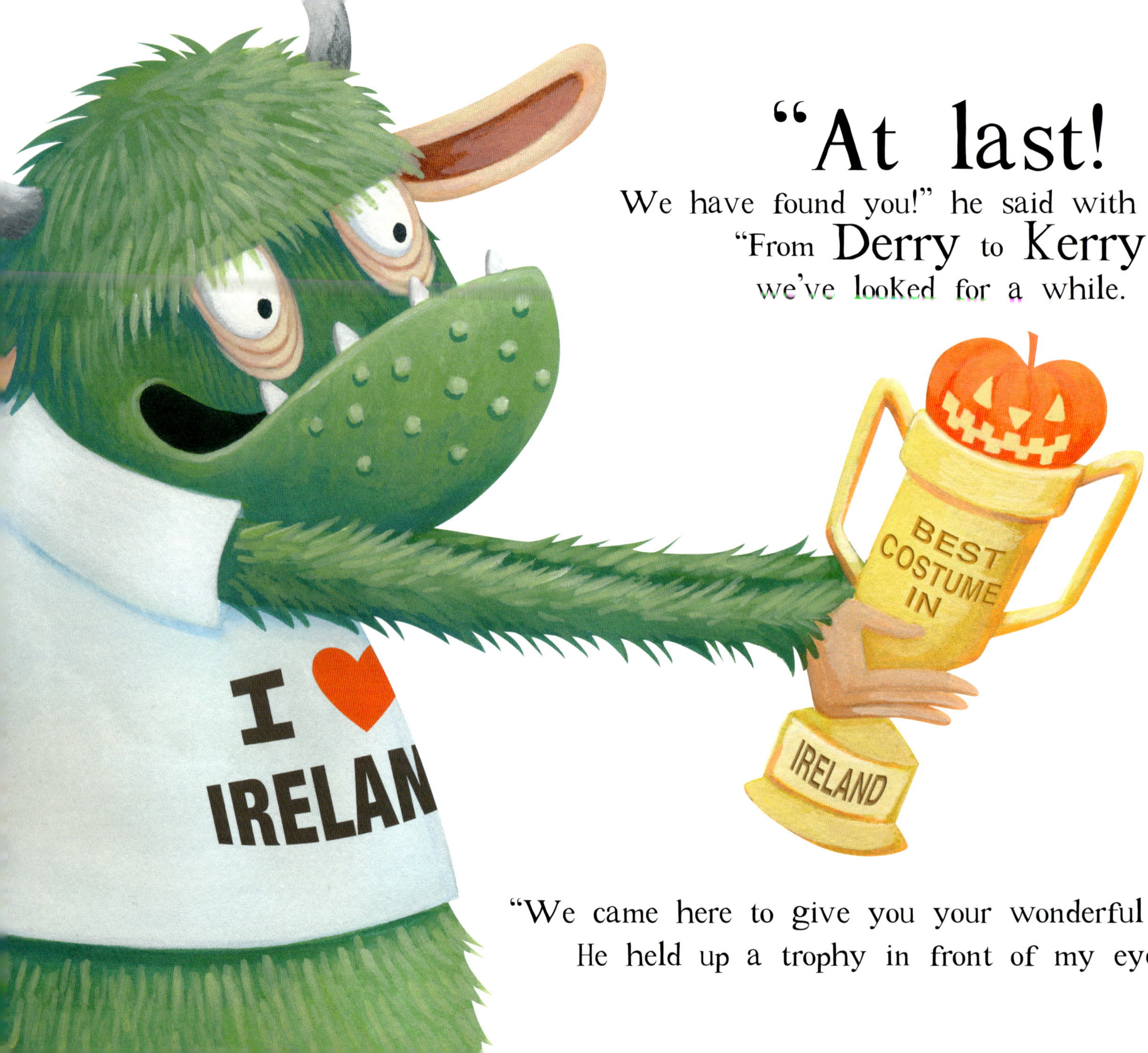

"We came here to give you your wonderful prize."
He held up a trophy in front of my eyes.

"A prize? And for me?"
I replied with a grin.
"But what did I enter and how did I win?"
"You've won the first prize for the costume you're wearing!
It even scares me, and I'm old-hat at scaring!"

"This isn't a costume. I'm just dressed as me!"

"Exactly, the scariest thing you can be!

A small human child, with a cute button nose.

Your teeth are so shiny, you've only ten toes.

No hair on your face and no horns on your head.

The whites of your eyes are not glowing or red!

A bone-chilling costume! A horrible sight!

A worthy ensemble for Halloween night!"

I ♥
IRELAND
BES
COSTUM
IN
IRELAND

We partied together
until the moon set,
A Halloween night
that I'll never forget.

And next year I won't
want to hide in my bed.
The monsters won't scare me...

I'll scare **THEM** instead!